## DATE DUE

# Learn to Fold Origami
# Zoo Animals

## Katie Gillespie

www.av2books.com

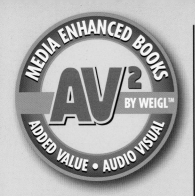

AV² provides enriched content that supplements and complements this book. Weigl's AV² books strive to create inspired learning and engage young minds in a total learning experience.

## Your AV² Media Enhanced books come alive with...

**Audio**
Listen to sections of the book read aloud.

**Key Words**
Study vocabulary, and complete a matching word activity.

**Video**
Watch informative video clips.

**Quizzes**
Test your knowledge.

**Embedded Weblinks**
Gain additional information for research.

**Slide Show**
View images and captions, and prepare a presentation.

**Try This!**
Complete activities and hands-on experiments.

**... and much, much more!**

Go to **www.av2books.com**, and enter this book's unique code.

**BOOK CODE**

**N 1 1 9 4 3 4**

**AV² by Weigl** brings you media enhanced books that support active learning.

Published by AV² by Weigl
350 5th Avenue, 59th Floor
New York, NY 10118
Website: www.weigl.com    www.av2books.com

Library of Congress Control Number: 2013939647

ISBN 978-1-62127-961-7 (Hardcover)
ISBN 978-1-62127-962-4 (Softcover)
ISBN 978-1-62127-963-1 (single user eBook)
ISBN 978-1-48960-035-6 (multi-user eBook)

Printed in the United States of America in North Mankato, Minnesota
1 2 3 4 5 6 7 8 9 0  17 16 15 14 13

062013
WEP220513

Senior Editor: Heather Kissock
Art Director: Terry Paulhus

Every reasonable effort has been made to trace ownership and to obtain permission to reprint copyright material. The publishers would be pleased to have any errors or omissions brought to their attention so that they may be corrected in subsequent printings.

Weigl acknowledges Getty Images as its primary image supplier for this title.

Origami patterns adapted from concepts originating with Fumiaki Shingu.

# Contents

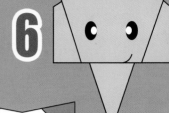

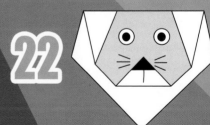

# Why Fold Origami?

**O**rigami is the Japanese art of paper folding. The Japanese, and the Chinese before them, have been folding paper into different shapes and designs for hundreds of years. The term "origami" comes from the Japanese words "ori," which means "folding," and "kami," which means "paper."

Paper used to be very expensive, so origami was an activity that only the rich could afford. Over time, paper became less expensive, and more people were able to participate in origami. Today, it is an art form that anyone can enjoy.

It is fun to make objects out of paper. Before you start doing origami, there are three basic folds that you must learn. Knowing these three folds will help you create almost any simple origami model.

## Hood Fold

Hood folds are often used to make an animal's head or neck. To make a hood fold, fold along the dotted line, and crease. Then, unfold the paper. Open the pocket you have created. Flip the paper inside out along the creases, and flatten.

## Pocket Fold

Pocket folds are often used to make an animal's mouth or tail. To make a pocket fold, fold along the dotted line, and crease. Then, unfold the paper. Open the pocket you have created. Fold the point inside along the creases, and flatten.

## Step Fold

Step folds are often used to make an animal's ears. To make a step fold, fold backward along the dotted line, and crease. Then, fold frontward along the dotted line, and crease. Repeat as necessary.

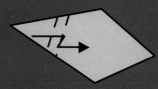

## You will need:

- Origami paper (or any square-shaped paper)
- Colored markers or crayons
- Safety scissors

Practice making your favorite zoo animals in this book to learn the skills needed to fold origami.

# Zoo Animals

**A** zoo is a place where animals are kept for public viewing. People visit zoos to see animals such as elephants, lions, and monkeys. Zoos serve a range of functions. They help scientists teach people about different types of animals found in the world. Zoos also protect **endangered** animals. Being in a zoo protects them from becoming **extinct**. It also allows their populations to grow by having babies.

Zoos do their best to recreate the animals' natural **habitats**. Doing so helps the animals feel more at home. It also helps people understand the types of places in which the animals thrive. People can learn about the animals and the **environment** by visiting a zoo.

As you fold the origami models in this book, consider the features of each zoo animal. Which features are unique and why? How would the zoo animal survive without these features?

# What Is an Elephant?

Adult elephants have 26 teeth, but they are not all present at the same time. New teeth grow in when older ones wear out. Their two tusks are also teeth. The tusks are made of ivory and can be up to 10 feet (3.4 meters) long. Elephants use their tusks for digging the ground in search of food.

Elephants are known for their huge size, strength, and intelligence. They are the world's largest living land animals. There are two kinds of elephants. One is the Asian elephant. The other is the African elephant. Each type is named for the continent where it lives in nature.

Elephants live in groups called herds. There are about 9 to 11 elephants in a herd. A herd is led by a female elephant. Elephants are social animals. They show affection by hugging each other with their trunks. They also rub their shoulders together. Elephants **communicate** through rumbling sounds. They sleep up to four hours every day.

**Trunk**

An elephant's trunk averages about 5 feet (1.5 meters) long. It can weigh up to 290 pounds (130 kg). With up to 150,000 muscles, the trunk has many uses. Elephants use their trunks to pick up food and other objects. They also suck up water with their trunks and blow it into their mouths to drink. Elephants use their trunks when they sense danger. They raise them in the air to sniff for information.

## Ears
An elephant's ears are large and thin at the tips. **Blood vessels** in the ears help control the elephant's body temperature. As the elephant flaps its ears, the air cools the blood in the vessels. The cooled blood then travels through the elephant's body.

## Skin
An elephant's skin is very thick, measuring up to 1 inch (2.5 cm) in some places. The skin is sensitive to sunlight. Elephants often cover themselves with mud to prevent their skin from drying out, cracking, or burning. The mud also protects them from insect bites or stings.

## Legs and Feet
An African elephant can weigh up to 18,000 pounds (8,000 kilograms). To support this weight, an elephant has strong legs and specially **adapted** feet. Each foot has a layer of padding between the toes and soles. When the elephant puts its weight on its foot, the padding helps absorb the shock.

# How to Fold an
# Elephant

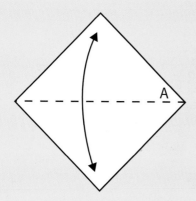

① Fold in half along line A, and crease. Open the paper.

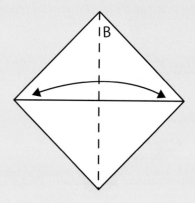

② Fold in half along line B, and crease. Open the paper.

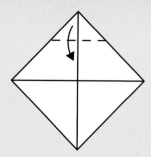

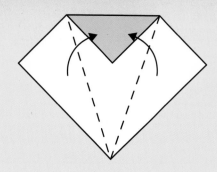

**3** Fold the top point down to meet the center line.

**4** Fold the right side in along the right dotted line, as shown. Repeat on the left side.

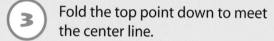

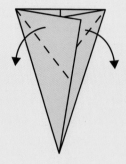

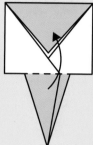

**5** Fold the left side down along the left dotted line, as shown. Repeat on the right side.

**6** Fold the bottom point up along the dotted line, as shown.

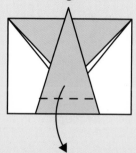

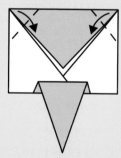

**7** To make the elephant's trunk, fold down along the dotted line, as shown.

**8** To make the elephant's ears, fold the left point in along the left dotted line, as shown. Repeat on the right side.

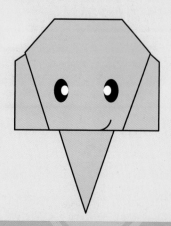

**9** Finish the elephant by turning it over and drawing its face.

# What Is a Giant Panda?

Giant pandas used to live in southern and eastern China, Myanmar, and North Vietnam. Today, they are found only in a small part of China. There are only about 1,600 giant pandas living in nature. Giant pandas are considered an endangered **species**. This is largely due to humans. People log the forests where pandas live to develop the land. As this happens, pandas lose their habitat.

Giant panda territories must contain bamboo to eat, thick bushes for shelter, and large, hollow fir trees for building dens. It is also very important for giant pandas to have a good source of drinking water nearby. Bamboo makes up 99 percent of a giant panda's diet. Pandas also eat grass, flowers, fruit, small animals, and some insects.

**Fur**
The giant panda's black-and-white markings most likely act like **camouflage**. The black around the eyes makes the eyes look bigger than they are. This may help scare off other animals.

## Face
A giant panda's face gets its round shape from its massive cheek muscles. These extremely strong muscles help pandas chew their bamboo.

## Teeth
Giant pandas have 42 teeth. Pandas use their teeth to peel off the tough outer layers of bamboo. Their molars are broad and flat. This tooth shape helps them to crush the shoots, leaves, and stems. Pandas also have strong jawbones.

## Paws
Giant pandas have five fingers and toes, and long, sharp claws that allow them to climb trees. The giant panda has a special enlarged wristbone. This acts like an **opposable thumb**. A panda can grasp a bamboo stalk by wrapping its fingers around the stalk and squeezing it against the wristbone to secure its hold.

# How to Fold a
# Giant Panda

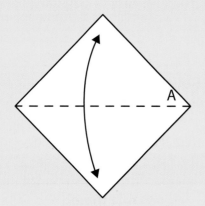

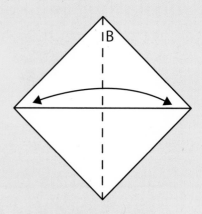

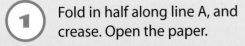 **1** Fold in half along line A, and crease. Open the paper.

**2** Fold in half along line B, and crease. Open the paper.

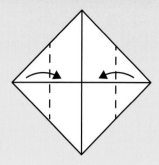

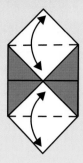

**3** Fold the left point in to meet the center line. Repeat on the right side.

**4** Fold the top point down to meet the center line, and crease. Open the paper. Repeat for the bottom point.

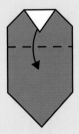

**5** Fold the top point backward along the dotted line, as shown.

**6** Turn the paper over. Then, fold the top down along the dotted line, as shown.

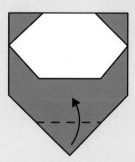

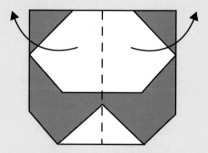

**7** Fold the bottom point up along the dotted line, as shown.

**8** Fold in half, and crease. Open the paper so the giant panda stands up.

**9** Finish the giant panda by drawing its eyes and nose.

# What Is a Giraffe?

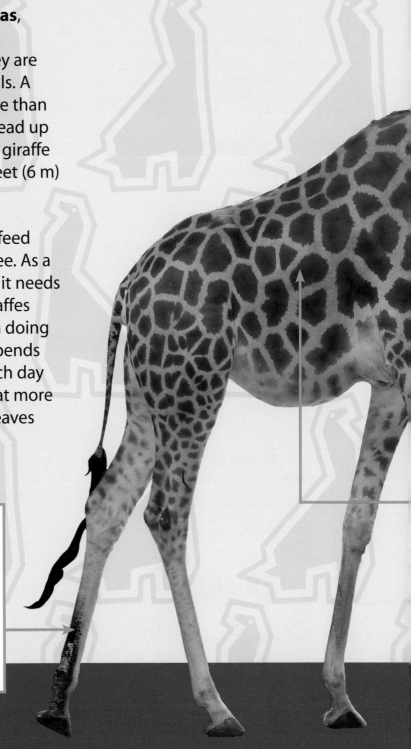

**G**iraffes live in the **savannas**, grasslands, and open woodlands of Africa. They are the world's tallest land animals. A male giraffe can stand at more than 18 feet (5.5 m). By lifting its head up and sticking out its tongue, a giraffe can eat greenery almost 20 feet (6 m) off the ground.

Giraffes use their tongues to feed on the leaves of the acacia tree. As a giraffe is such a large animal, it needs plenty of food to survive. Giraffes spend more time eating than doing any other activity. A giraffe spends between 16 and 20 hours each day feeding. An adult male will eat more than 145 pounds (65 kg) of leaves and twigs in a day.

### Legs and Feet

A giraffe's legs are up to 6 feet (1.8 m) long. Even though the back legs look shorter, they are almost the same length as the front legs. A giraffe's feet are 12 inches (30 cm) across. Giraffes can run up to 31 miles (50 km) per hour over distance.

## Neck

A giraffe's neck can be up to 6 feet (1.8 m) long and weigh as much as 600 pounds (272 kg). As long as a giraffe's neck is, it still has the same number of **vertebrae** as a human's neck.

## Horns

Both male and female giraffes have horns. The horns are made of bone and are covered with skin and hair. The tops of the horns are rounded, not sharp. They can be up to 9 inches (23 cm) long and 6 inches (15 cm) around.

## Eyes

Giraffes have excellent eyesight, and because of their height, they can spot **predators** at great distances. Some giraffes are able to see up to 1 mile (1.6 km) away. Like other animals, giraffes are more likely to see something that moves rather than something standing still. Giraffes are also able to tell the difference between colors.

## Pattern

Giraffes have patterns of light to dark brown markings on a cream-colored background. Each giraffe's pattern is unique. Giraffe species are divided based on the pattern of their fur.

# Giraffe

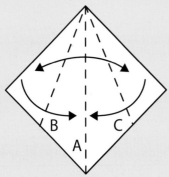

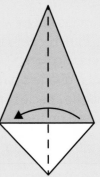

① Fold in half along line A, and crease. Open the paper. Then, fold along lines B and C to meet the center line, as shown.

② Fold in half along the dotted line. Then, turn the paper.

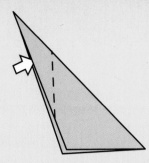

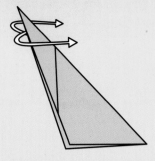

**3** Fold along the dotted line, as shown, and crease. Unfold the paper and open the pocket at the white arrow.

**4** To make the giraffe's neck, make a hood fold, as shown.

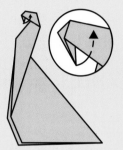

**5** To make the giraffe's head, fold along the dotted line, and crease. Then, unfold the paper and make a hood fold, as shown.

**6** To make the giraffe's mouth, make a pocket fold at the tip, as shown.

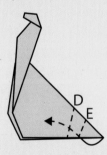

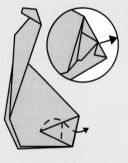

**7** Fold along line D, and crease. Unfold the paper. Then, make a pocket fold along line E, as shown.

**8** To make the giraffe's tail, make a pocket fold, and pull out the tip, as shown.

**9** Finish the giraffe by cutting out its legs and drawing its eyes and pattern.

# What Is a Hippopotamus?

**H**ippopotamuses are large **mammals** that live in the rivers and swamps of Africa. Hippopotamuses are often called "hippos" for short. Hippos live in groups, or herds, of about 15. They have a life span of up to 50 years.

Hippos are amphibious. This means they live both on land and in water. Hippos spend most of their day in the water. This helps keep their temperature down. Hippos come onto land at night to eat. They are **herbivores** and can eat up to 80 pounds (35 kg) of grass each night. Hippos also drink plenty of water. They drink about 56 gallons (250 liters) of water each day.

### Skin
Hippos are grayish-brown in color. A hippo's skin is very thick, especially over its back and rump. Its hide alone can weigh 0.5 ton (454 kg).

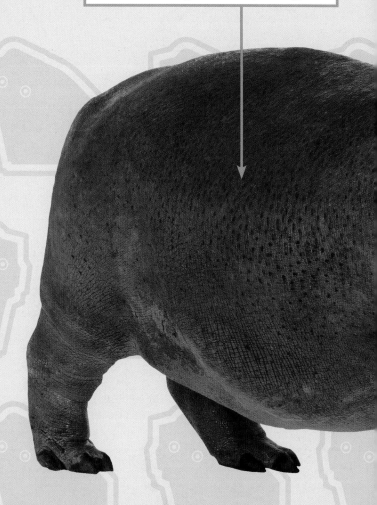

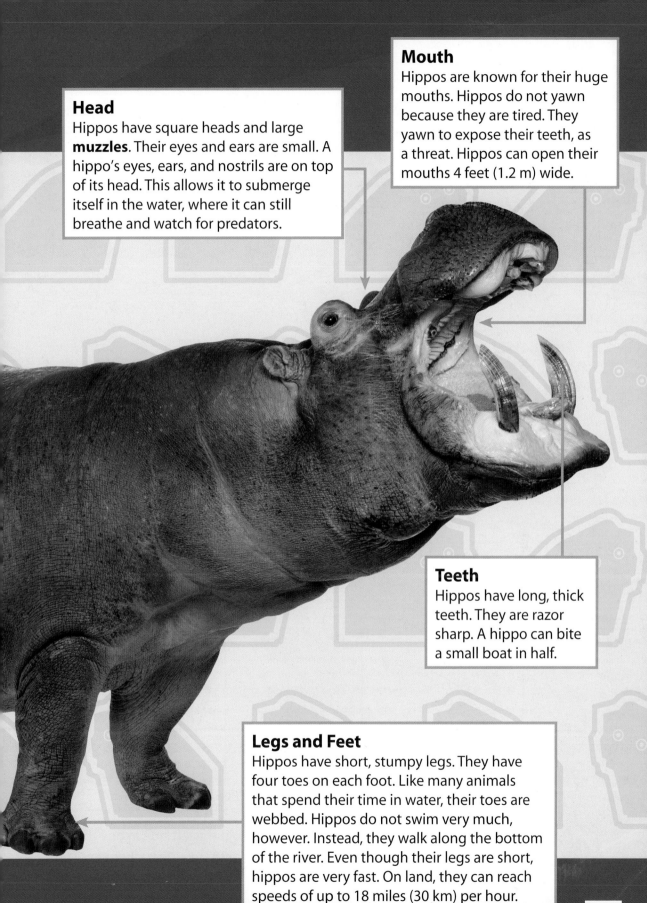

## Head
Hippos have square heads and large **muzzles**. Their eyes and ears are small. A hippo's eyes, ears, and nostrils are on top of its head. This allows it to submerge itself in the water, where it can still breathe and watch for predators.

## Mouth
Hippos are known for their huge mouths. Hippos do not yawn because they are tired. They yawn to expose their teeth, as a threat. Hippos can open their mouths 4 feet (1.2 m) wide.

## Teeth
Hippos have long, thick teeth. They are razor sharp. A hippo can bite a small boat in half.

## Legs and Feet
Hippos have short, stumpy legs. They have four toes on each foot. Like many animals that spend their time in water, their toes are webbed. Hippos do not swim very much, however. Instead, they walk along the bottom of the river. Even though their legs are short, hippos are very fast. On land, they can reach speeds of up to 18 miles (30 km) per hour.

# How to Fold a
# Hippopotamus

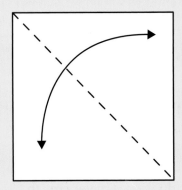

**1** Fold in half along the dotted line, and crease. Open the paper.

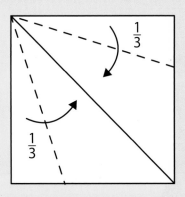

**2** Fold the left side in one third along the dotted line, as shown. Repeat on the top.

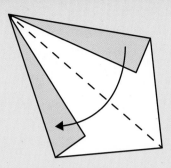

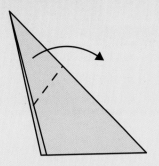

**3** Fold in half lengthwise, as shown..

**4** Fold the top down along the dotted line, as shown.

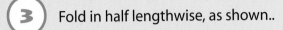
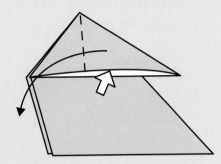

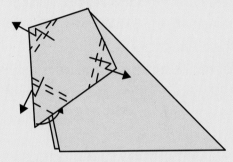

**5** Open the pocket at the white arrow, and flatten.

**6** Fold the tip backward along the dotted line. Step fold along the bottom line, as shown. Repeat on the left and right points.

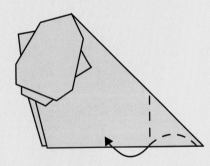

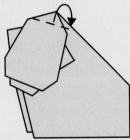

**7** Fold along the dotted line, and crease. Unfold the paper. Then, make a pocket fold, as shown.

**8** Fold the top backward along the dotted line, as shown.

**9** Finish the hippopotamus by cutting out its legs and drawing its eyes.

# What Is a Lion?

Lions are large wild cats that live in the savannas, grasslands, and open woodlands of Africa. There are about 6,000 to 10,000 lions in Africa. Most of them live on protected reserves. Lions have a life span of about 15 years in nature. In a zoo, a lion can live up to 30 years.

Lions live in groups called prides. A pride has 15 lions on average, including females, babies, and a few adult males. Male lions are simply called lions. Female lions are called lionesses. Baby lions are called cubs. Lionesses give birth to cubs every two years. They have between one and six cubs at a time. Lion cubs can be targets for predators. Only about 30 percent of lion cubs survive their first two years.

### Mouth
Lions have strong jaws and 30 sharp teeth. The long, sharply pointed teeth at the front are used to hold on to and kill **prey**. The back teeth work like scissors to slice flesh. Rough, hook-like structures on the tongue work like sandpaper to help lions strip bits of meat from bones.

## Eyes

With their large, golden-amber eyes, lions see about as well as humans during the day. At night, however, their pupils can open very wide—about three times bigger than the pupils of human eyes. This lets them collect light even when it is dark. The more light their eyes gather, the better lions can see and hunt in the dark.

## Mane

Only male lions have a mane. This distinguishes them from females. A lion gets its mane at about age three. It continues to grow until age five. The mane protects a lion's neck when it fights other animals. It is reddish-brown to black in color. The darker a lion's mane, the more likely he is to attract a mate.

## Paws

Soft pads on the bottom of a lion's paws help cushion and muffle each step as lions stalk their prey. Razor-sharp, curved claws help lions bring down prey and prevent it from escaping. Like all cats, lions have **retractable claws** that are kept in unless they are needed.

# How to Fold a
# Lion

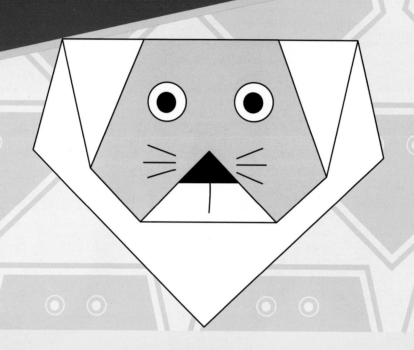

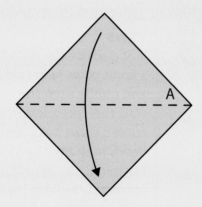

**1** Fold in half along line A, and crease.

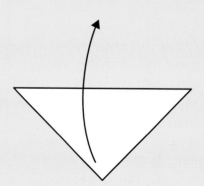

**2** Open the paper.

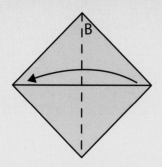

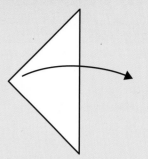

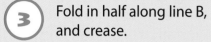

**3** Fold in half along line B, and crease.

**4** Open the paper.

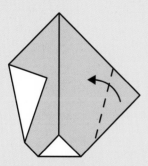

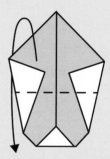

**5** Fold the bottom point up along the dotted line, as shown.

**6** Fold the left point in along the dotted line, as shown.

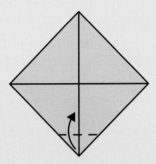

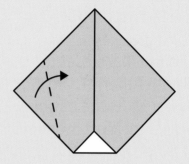

**7** Fold the right point in along the dotted line, as shown.

**8** Fold backward along the dotted line, as shown.

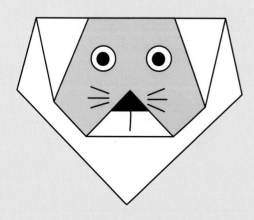

**9** Finish the lion by drawing its eyes, nose, and whiskers.

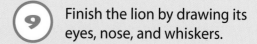

# What Is a Monkey?

There are 200 known species of monkey. Monkeys can be divided into two groups. New World monkeys, including the marmoset, live in South America. Old World monkeys, such as the baboon, live in Asia and Africa. Most monkeys live in trees. Some live on the ground. Some species can live up to 50 years in nature.

Monkeys are very social. Most live in groups called "troops." Being in a troop is important to monkeys. When they are young, the troop gives them a safe, secure place in which to grow. With up to 100 monkeys, a troop can protect itself from predators better than a lone monkey can. Food may be easier to find in a troop as well because each troop has its own favorite feeding spots.

## Tail

A monkey's tail can be up to 35 inches (89 cm) long. However, some monkeys have no tail at all. The tail is often used like another arm. Monkeys can wrap it around branches and other objects. The top of a monkey's tail is furry. The underside is ridged. This helps give the monkey a better grip.

## Eyes

Monkeys have two large, forward-facing eyes. They can judge distance and depth while moving and can sharply focus on movement around them. Like humans, monkeys can see in color.

## Teeth

Monkeys have either 32 or 36 teeth, depending on whether it is an Old World or New World monkey. Two canine teeth at the front of the mouth are used for tearing food. Other teeth are used for biting, slicing, grinding, and crushing food. Some monkeys have cheek pouches that they use to store food.

## Hands and Feet

Most monkeys have four flexible fingers and an opposable thumb. This lets them pinch their fingers and thumbs together to grasp things. Monkeys have tiny, raised ridges on their fingertips that help them feel and grip objects. A monkey's feet are much like its hands. This means monkeys can also grip objects with their feet.

# Monkey

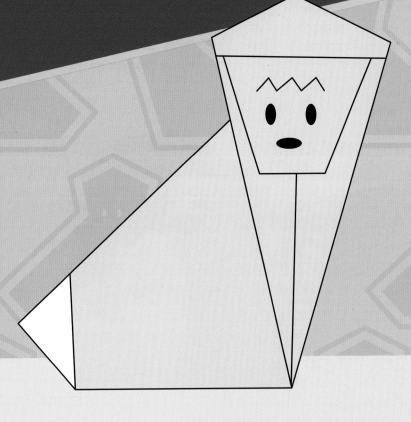

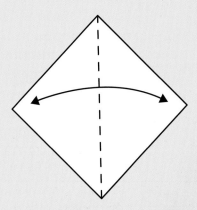

1. Fold in half along the dotted line, and crease. Open the paper.

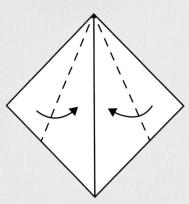

2. Fold the left side in along the dotted line to meet the center line. Repeat on the right side.

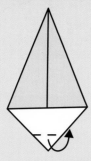

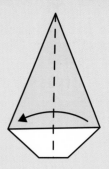

**3** Fold the bottom point backward along the dotted line, as shown.

**4** Fold in half along the dotted line. Then, turn the paper.

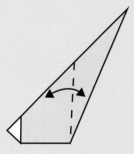

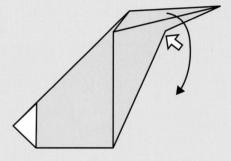

**5** Fold along the dotted line, and crease. Unfold the paper.

**6** Open the pocket at the white arrow, and flatten.

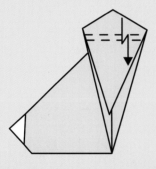

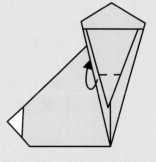

**7** To make the monkey's head, step fold along the dotted line, as shown.

**8** Fold the tip backward along the dotted line, as shown.

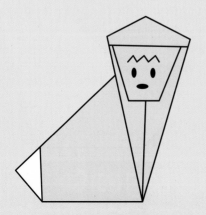

**9** Finish the monkey by drawing its face.

# Test Your Knowledge of Zoo Animals

**1.**

What are an elephant's tusks made of?

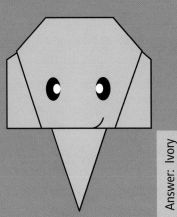

Answer: Ivory

**2.**

What makes up 99 percent of a giant panda's diet?

Answer: Bamboo

**3.**

How long is a giraffe's neck?

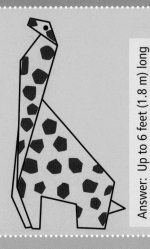

Answer: Up to 6 feet (1.8 m) long

**4.**

How long do hippos live?

Answer: Up to 50 years

**5.**

What color is a lion's mane?

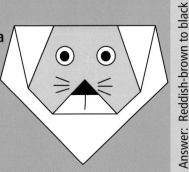

Answer: Reddish-brown to black

**6.**

What is the name for a group of monkeys?

Answer: A troop

Want to learn more? Log on to www.av2books.com to access more content.

# Zoo Animal Fact Game

**Materials**
- Crayons or markers
- Several sheets of blank paper
- Reusable cloth shopping bag
- 2 or more friends

**Steps**

1. As a group, brainstorm a list of as many zoo animals as possible. List them on a piece of paper.
2. Using your crayons or markers, draw one picture of each zoo animal on separate sheets of paper. Write the numbers 1 through 5 on the back of each sheet.
3. Fold each drawing in half. Put all of your drawings inside the bag, and shake it around to mix them up.
4. Take turns pulling papers from the bag. For each drawing you pull, think of a fact about that animal. Write your fact on the back of the drawing. Then, return it to the bag of animals.
5. Keep choosing animals from the bag and listing fun facts until you have come up with five for each animal. How many different zoo animal facts do you know?

# Key Words

**adapted:** changed in order to make suitable

**blood vessels:** any of the tubes in the body through which blood flows

**camouflage:** a disguise used to hide something by making it look like its surroundings

**communicate:** to exchange information

**endangered:** at risk of no longer living on Earth

**environment:** the living things and conditions of a particular place

**extinct:** no longer living on Earth

**habitats:** the environment in which an animal lives

**herbivores:** animals that eat only plants

**mammals:** animals that are warm-blooded and have a backbone

**muzzles:** the nose, mouth, and jaws of an animal

**opposable thumb:** a thumb that can bend to grasp something

**predators:** animals that hunt other animals for food

**prey:** animals that are hunted as food

**retractable claws:** claws that can be pulled into the paw

**savannas:** flat, grassy plains

**species:** animals that share common traits

**vertebrae:** the small bones in the backbone

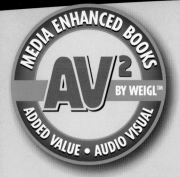

# Log on to www.av2books.com

AV² by Weigl brings you media enhanced books that support active learning. Go to www.av2books.com, and enter the special code found on page 2 of this book. You will gain access to enriched and enhanced content that supplements and complements this book. Content includes video, audio, weblinks, quizzes, a slide show, and activities.

## AV² Online Navigation

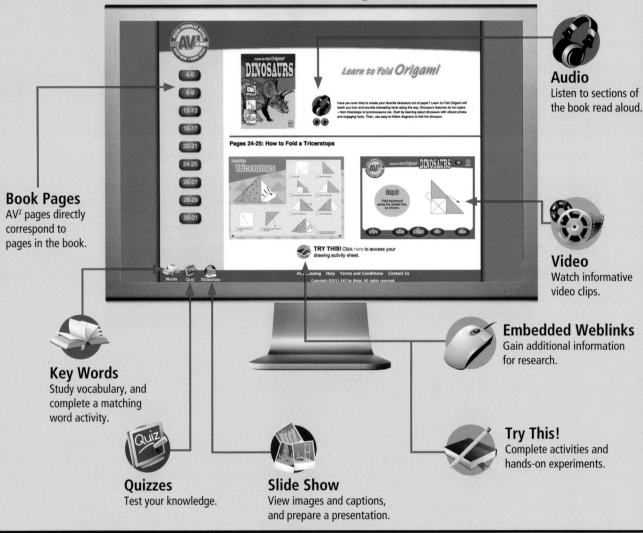

**Book Pages**
AV² pages directly correspond to pages in the book.

**Audio**
Listen to sections of the book read aloud.

**Video**
Watch informative video clips.

**Embedded Weblinks**
Gain additional information for research.

**Key Words**
Study vocabulary, and complete a matching word activity.

**Try This!**
Complete activities and hands-on experiments.

**Quizzes**
Test your knowledge.

**Slide Show**
View images and captions, and prepare a presentation.

AV² was built to bridge the gap between print and digital. We encourage you to tell us what you like and what you want to see in the future.

## Sign up to be an AV² Ambassador at www.av2books.com/ambassador.